THE LAND AND RESOURCES OF COLORADO

Mark Laney

NEW YORK

Published in 2016 by The Rosen Publishing Group, Inc.
29 East 21st Street, New York, NY 10010

Editor: Debbie Nevins
Book Design: Iron Cupcake Design

Cataloging-in-Publication Data

Laney, Mark.
The land and resources of Colorado / by Mark Laney.
p. cm. — (Spotlight on Colorado)
Includes index.
ISBN 978-1-4994-1438-7 (pbk.)
ISBN 978-1-4994-1439-4 (6 pack)
ISBN 978-1-4994-1441-7 (library binding)
1. Colorado — Juvenile literature. 2. Colorado — Geography — Juvenile literature. I. Laney, Mark. II. Title.
F776.3 L364 2016
978.8—d23

Photo Credits: Don Mammoser/Shutterstock.com, cover; © iStockphoto.com/FrankRamspott, cover (inset); shaferaphoto/Shutterstock.com, 3; chrupka/Shutterstock.com, 4; Sarah Fields Photography/Shutterstock.com, 5; marekuliasz/Shutterstock.com, 5; DUCEPT Pascal/hemis.fr/Getty Images, 6; Westend61/Getty Images, 7; Gary Conner/Stockbyte/Getty Images, 8; Theshibboleth/File:US Great Plains Map.svg/Wikimedia Commons, 9; silky/Shutterstock.com, 10; Tom Reichner/Shutterstock.com, 10; Todd Shoemake/Shutterstock.com, 11; Pete Saloutos/Getty Images, 13; Bardocz Peter/Shutterstock.com, 15; Ericshawwhite/File:Sonia & Gunter.JPG/Wikimedia Commons, 16; Patrick Poendl/Shutterstock.com, 16; Pfly/File:NorthAmericaWaterDivides.png/Wikimedia Commons, 17; Phillip Rubino/Shutterstock.com, 18; Andy Magee/Shutterstock.com, 19; WorldPictures/Shutterstock.com, 20; Dorling Kindersley/Dorling Kindersley/Getty Images, 21; Oscity/Shutterstock.com, 22; Steve Shoup/Shutterstock.com, 23; Claudio Del Luongo/Shutterstock.com, 24; Janis Maleckis/Shutterstock.com, 25; Peter Kunasz/Shutterstock.com, 25; Arina P Habich/Shutterstock.com, 26; Pete Mcbride/National Geographic/Getty Images, 27; Stephen Saks/Lonely Planet Images/Getty Images, 28; Comstock/Stockbyte/Getty Images, 29; David Parsons/E+/Getty Images, 30; Mark Hayes/Shutterstock.com, 30; David Wall Photo/Lonely Planet Images/Getty Images, 31; Tyler Stableford/The Image Bank/Getty Images, 32; Glenn Asakawa/The Denver Post via Getty Images, 34; Walter Bibikow/AWL Images/Getty Images, 34; JimIrwin/File:Colorado population map.png/Wikimedia Commons, 35; John Hoffman/Shutterstock.com, 36; Arina P Habich/Shutterstock.com, 36; Ed Freeman/Photodisc/Getty Images, 37; Gert Hochmuth/Shutterstock.com, 38; Doug Meek/Shutterstock.com, 39; Alexey Kamenskiy/Shutterstock.com, 40; Russell Burden/Getty Images, 41; Ryan DeBerardinis/Shutterstock.com, 41; Larsek/Shutterstock.com, 42; Thomas Barrat/Shutterstock.com, 42; Arina P Habich/Shutterstock.com, 43; Tom Reichner/Shutterstock.com, 44; Kane513/Shutterstock.com, 44; Volt Collection/Shutterstock.com, 44; Tom Reichner/Shutterstock.com, 44; welcomia/Shutterstock.com, 45.

Manufactured in the United States of America

CPSIA Compliance Information: Batch #BS15PK: For further information contact Rosen Publishing, New York, New York at 1-800-237-9932

Contents

CHAPTER 1

A Colorful Land

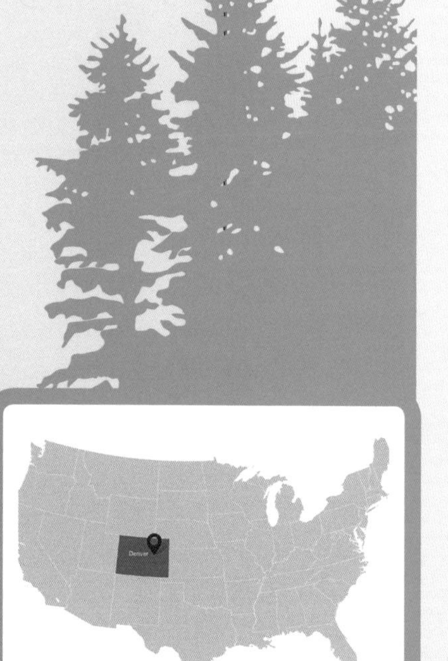

A RECTANGULAR SHAPE

Colorado is one of only three states—along with Utah and Wyoming—whose borders are completely defined by map lines of latitude and longitude rather than by natural land formations.

It's easy to guess that Colorado is a very colorful place—its name tells us so! *Colorado* is a Spanish word meaning "red" or "color." Early Spanish explorers of this part of North America were impressed by the red sandstone soil and rocky red cliffs they found here. In certain places, red sediment flows into the rivers. Some historians say the explorers used the word *colorado* to describe the mighty river that flows down from the Rocky Mountains. The name of the territory, they say, came from the river. However this state first got its name, it's a good one, because Colorado is colorful in many ways.

Colorado, which became a state in 1876, is in the western part of the United States. It is the eighth-largest state in size, but only the 22nd in terms of population. It covers three major geographical regions—the Great Plains, Rocky Mountains, and Colorado Plateau—that

The sandstone cliffs of Pikes Peak glow red in the morning sun.

feature a wide variety of landforms. This state has craggy mountains, flat grasslands, dense forests, deserts, canyons, and **mesas**. Mesas are flat-topped mountains. The state also has many natural resources. They include oil, natural gas, coal, rivers, and minerals such as gold and silver.

In this book, we'll look at how Colorado's land and resources shaped its growth.

Colorado's beautiful scenery is an important resource. Tourists come from all over to see the state's unusual landforms and dramatic mountain vistas.

CHAPTER 2

Colorado's Geographical Regions

Three major land areas roughly divide the state: the High Plains of the east, the mountains of the west central section, and the mesa country of the Western Slope, part of the Colorado Plateau. Within these regions, there are smaller areas of geographical distinction.

For example, the Colorado Front Range lies just east of the Rocky Mountain foothills. It's where the prairie meets the mountains and is a broad, hilly valley. Most of the state's major cities are in this region, including Denver.

The Colorado Plateau is a land region that extends far beyond the borders of Colorado. It also covers large sections of New Mexico, Arizona, and Utah.

THE COLORADO PLATEAU

SHELTER ME!

The Rocky Mountains partially protect the Front Range region from storms that blow in from the Pacific Ocean farther west.

Denver sits on a flat area where the High Plains meet the Front Range. The Rocky Mountains are in the distance.

	Western Slope	Rocky Mountains	High Plains
Where	western Colorado	west central, running north-south	eastern Colorado
Features	hills, deep valleys, mesas	mountains, rivers, the Continental Divide	flat prairie, rising gently from east to west
Weather Conditions	dry hot summers, sunny cold winters	cool, dry air; very cold, snowy winters	dry air, hot summers, cold winters, windy springs, little rainfall, hail and thunderstorms
Resources	oil shale, natural gas, oil, forests, the Colorado River	very high mountain peaks, waterfalls, lakes, national parks, scenic highways, oil shale	grasslands, rich soils
Economy	fruit orchards, health care, energy mining	tourism, skiing	farming, livestock

CHAPTER 3

The High Plains

When most people think of Colorado, they think of mountains. But the entire eastern part of the state is as flat as a pancake. (In fact, some scientists once figured out that neighboring Kansas is actually *flatter* than a pancake!)

Welcome to the High Plains. Here you can travel for miles on long, straight highways and see treeless fields right out to the horizon. You

Eastern Colorado is so flat that on a clear day you can see Pikes Peak all the way from Kansas—or so they say.

Shortgrass prairie—(High Plains)
Midgrass prairie
Tallgrass prairie

might also see grain silos, grazing cattle, and the occasional small town, but no big cities.

Are you in the middle of nowhere? No, you are somewhere pretty *great*—the Great Plains!

The Mississippi River runs right down the center of the United States, dividing the country in two. To the west of the river lies a vast expanse of flat, grassy lands.

KNOWLEDGE NUGGET

The High Plains is one of the least densely populated regions in the United States.

They extend about 500 miles (805 kilometers) from the Mississippi to the Rocky Mountains. They stretch from Canada to Mexico—a distance of about 2,000 miles (3,219 km). Altogether, this flat prairie land is called the Great Plains.

PRAIRIE, YES; DOG, NO!

Prairie dogs are not dogs. They are rabbit-size rodents that live in the grassy plains. The animals dig burrows under the ground. Some people think they are cute, but farmers and ranchers consider them pests. During the 20th century, about 98 percent of the prairie dog population was destroyed.

The High Plains lie within the so-called Tornado Alley. That's a section of the country that is particularly prone to tornadoes.

A tornado touches down in southeastern Colorado.

These grassy lands continue from Kansas and Nebraska into eastern Colorado. Here they are called the High Plains because of their elevation. The land slowly rises from east to west in elevation until it meets the Rocky Mountains. Colorado's plains rise from about 3,400 feet (1,128 m) in elevation at the state's eastern border with Kansas to 7,500 feet (2,286 m) high east of Denver.

CHAPTER 4

Rocky Mountains

TAKE THAT, ALASKA!
Colorado has the highest average altitude of all the states.

Traveling westward, it seems like the High Plains bump right into a wall of soaring, jagged **peaks**. These are the Rocky Mountains, one of the major ranges in North America. The Rockies, as they are called, extend in a ragged north–south direction for some 3,000 miles (4,828 km), from Canada to the southwestern United States. Along the way, the range runs directly through central and western Colorado and into New Mexico.

Unlike the mountain ranges in the eastern part of North America, the Rockies are taller, craggy peaks that rise high above the tree line. Many are snowcapped year-round.

KNOWLEDGE NUGGET

The Rockies are usually divided into five sections: the Southern Rockies, Middle Rockies, Northern Rockies, the Brooks Range in Alaska (all in the United States),and the Rocky Mountain System in Canada.

In autumn, golden aspen trees shimmer against the snowy peaks.

SING IT!

"Rocky Mountain High," a popular song by longtime Colorado resident John Denver, is one of Colorado's two official state songs.

In Colorado, 53 mountains rise above 14,000 feet (4,267 m) above sea level. Mountaineers call such high peaks "fourteeners."

Mount Elbert, at 14,433 feet (4,399 m) is the highest summit, or mountaintop, in Colorado. It's also the highest Rocky Mountain peak in North America. This massive giant is in a section of the Rockies called the Sawatch Range.

The Rocky Mountains have played a crucial role in Colorado's history, culture, and economy. Years ago, the mountains posed a difficult barrier to explorers and settlers moving west across the continent. Then the peaks revealed their hidden treasures—gold, silver, and other metals and minerals, as well as oil and gas. Today the Rockies attract tourists to see the magnificent scenery and enjoy skiing, mountain climbing, and other activities.

The Rocky Mountain Range actually represents a series of more than 100 separate mountain ranges, rather than one uninterrupted mountain chain.

Nearly 20 rivers have their sources in Colorado, with the Continental Divide directing each river's course.

CHAPTER 5

Continental Divide

The Rocky Mountains are fascinating for many reasons. For one, they form the Continental Divide in North America. This invisible line runs from northern Alaska right down to the tip of the South American continent. Along the way, the Continental Divide passes through western Canada and the United States. Its zigzag course crosses the tops of Colorado's highest peaks.

CONTINENTAL DIVIDE TRAIL

Each year, about 200 people try to hike the trail's entire length. The trek can take about six months!

Travelers journey on horseback on the Continental Trail.

WRANGLE UP SOME FACTS

Winter lasts about nine months on the Continental Divide, with dangerous conditions from September to May.

Also called "The Great Divide," this line splits the continent into two giant **watersheds**. All rivers that arise west of the divide drain to the Pacific Ocean. Rivers that begin east of the line drain to the Atlantic Ocean. This doesn't mean all rivers run directly to those oceans, but their waters will eventually end up there. Rivers flow into other rivers, or other bodies of water, and so on, until they reach the ocean.

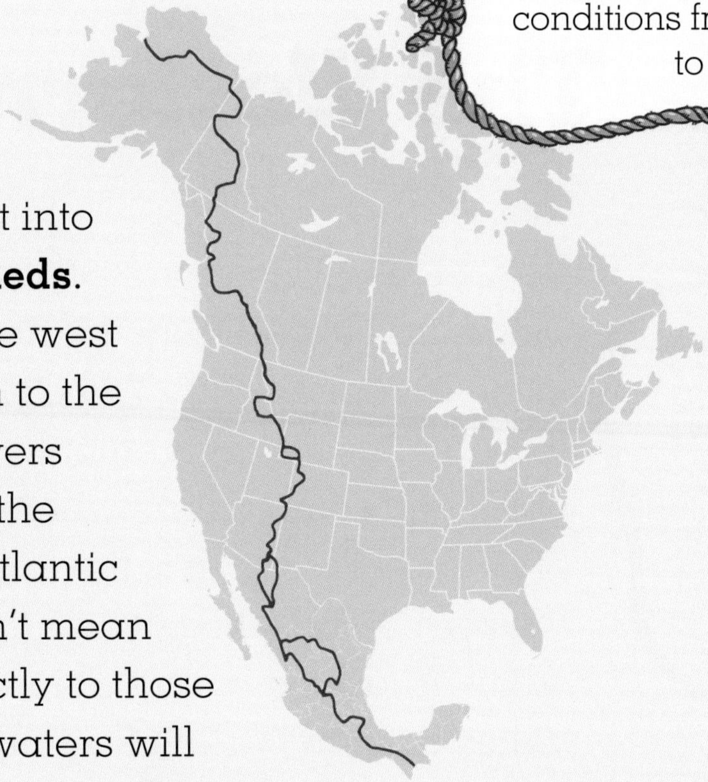

The red line shows the Continental Divide in North America.

In Colorado, the Continental Divide plays another role as well. A hiking route follows it through some of the state's wildest and highest territory. The Continental Divide National Scenic Trail extends about 3,100 miles (5,000 km) from Canada to Mexico. It passes through Montana, Idaho, Wyoming, Colorado, and New Mexico.

CHAPTER 6

The Western Slope

Grand Junction enjoys a milder winter than the rest of Colorado, a fact that helped encourage people to settle here.

West of the Continental Divide is the Western Slope. It stretches from the Rocky Mountains to the border of Utah. The Colorado River runs through this rugged region, dividing it into north and south. That's where you find the city of Grand Junction. It is the largest city on the Western Slope. The city lies in the Grand Valley, which is formed by the Colorado River. This valley is an important fruit-growing region and has a large number of orchards.

Orchards and vineyards grow at the foot of a mesa on the Western Slope.

KNOWLEDGE NUGGET

The Black Canyon is 48 miles (77 km) long! Its name comes from the fact that its walls are often shrouded in shadows, making them appear black.

THE BLACK CANYON

Western Colorado is an area of spectacular landforms. No wonder so many place-names include the word "grand"! It is a land of mesas, canyons, and high desert flatlands. Mesas are flat-topped mountains with sides of steep, colorful rock. Grand Mesa, southeast of Grand Junction, is the largest flat-topped mountain in the world. It rises about 6,000 feet (1,829 m) above the valleys and is about 40 miles (64 km) long.

Canyons are deep, dramatic breaks in the land. Rock-faced cliffs line both sides of the break. A river or dry riverbed often runs along the bottom. Probably the best known canyon in the United States is the Grand Canyon in Arizona. In Colorado, however, the Black Canyon, with the Gunnison River far, far below, is an awesome sight. The view can give you goosebumps!

WHERE THE DINOS ROAMED

Dinosaur National Park is a U.S. National Monument on the border of Colorado and Utah. Dinosaur fossil beds were discovered here in 1909.

CHAPTER 7

The San Luis Valley

In south central Colorado lies the San Luis Valley. This high, mostly flat region lies between the Sangre de Cristo Mountains, or the East Range, on the east, and the San Juan Mountains on the west. Both of these very high, rugged ranges are part of the Rocky Mountains. The valley itself, which extends a bit into New Mexico to the south, is more than 7,000 feet (2,134 m) in altitude. It runs about 122 miles (196 km) from north to south and about 74 miles (119 km) from east to west.

It's an **alpine** desert environment, and parts of it are very dry. It gets very little precipitation.

RING AROUND THE VALLEY

The San Luis Valley is ringed on all sides by mountains, which has made it a relatively isolated place. Crestone Peak, left, in the Sangre de Cristo Range, is seen here from Great Sand Dunes National Park.

The town of San Luis, located in the valley of the same name, is the oldest continually occupied town in Colorado.

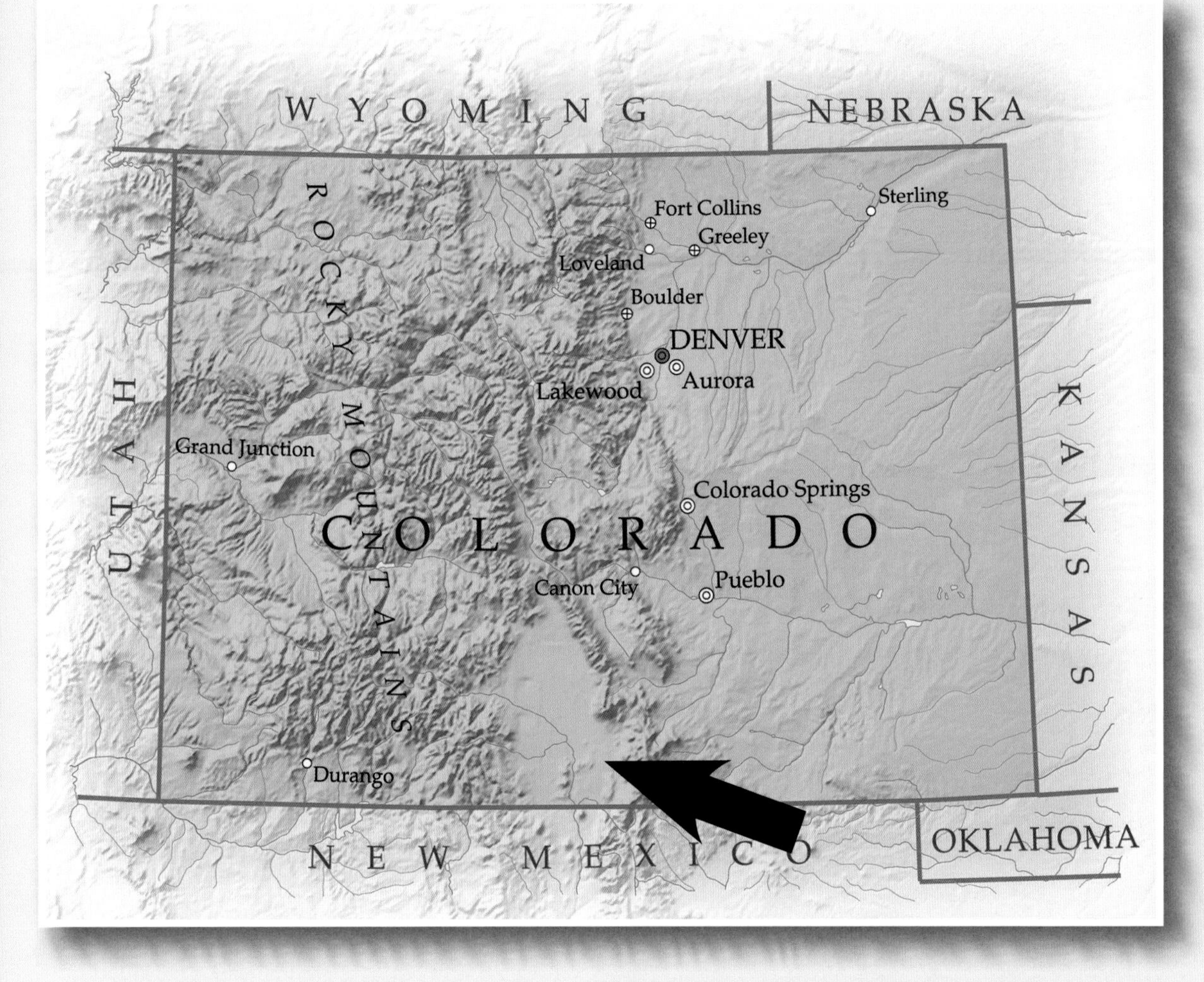

The map shows the rugged terrain of the Rocky Mountains. The arrow points to the high, flat San Luis Valley. You can see how the valley is surrounded by mountains.

Colorado averages 300 days of sunshine each year.

The land is widely covered with low brushy growth such as rabbitbrush, greasewood, and other woody species.

Originally the valley was home to the native Ute people. Farmers and ranchers from New Mexico settled here in the mid-1800s. They built irrigation canals to capture the waters flowing down from the surrounding mountains and divert them to the valley. With irrigation, the southern part of the valley supports agriculture. Crops such as potatoes, lettuce, barley, and quinoa grow here.

The valley is the location of several tourist attractions, including the Great Sand Dunes National Park and Preserve (left). Fort Garland, known as the "Gateway to the San Luis Valley," is home to a community of artists, craftspeople, and musicians.

Shrubby brush often covers uncultivated land in the San Luis Valley.

CHAPTER 8

Rivers

The Taylor River rises in the Elk Mountains near the Continental Divide.

Rivers are the lifeblood of a place. Their waters bring life to the land by supporting both plants and animals. Imagine if Colorado had no rivers! For one thing, people wouldn't live here; the land would be an empty desert. But of course, native people have lived here

THE TAYLOR RIVER

THE BLUE MESA RESERVOIR IN GUNNISON

for thousands of years. The rivers provided people with water, food, and a means of transportation. The same is true today.

Colorado's major rivers arise in the Rocky Mountains. They flow east or west according to which side of the Continental Divide they begin on. In the eastern plains, the major waterways are the South Platte and the Arkansas Rivers. They have numerous **tributaries**, or smaller branch rivers, that feed them. These rivers allow the Great Plains to support farming and ranching.

The Rio Grande is a river which rises in southern Colorado. Just don't call it the Rio Grande River, because *Rio* means "river" in Spanish!

HUNGRY?

The Fryingpan River is a tributary of the Roaring Fork River. Both are in western Colorado. The Fryingpan is famous for its fly-fishing—a hint to what ends up in the frying pan.

A fisherman casts a fly in the Taylor River.

Along certain stretches of these waterways, where trout are plentiful, fly-fishing is a popular sport.

In the west, the Colorado River flows southwest from its **headwaters** high up in the Rockies. It rushes down through the rugged **terrain** of the Western Slope. Then it comes to the rich farmlands of the Grand Valley. At Grand Junction, the river meets the Gunnison River, one of its largest tributaries. Gaining strength and growing bigger as it goes along, the river then flows through a high desert region and into neighboring Utah.

DON'T LOOK DOWN!

The Royal Gorge Bridge, the highest suspension bridge in the United States, spans the Arkansas River near Cañon City at a height of 1,053 feet (321 m).

The Colorado River is the seventh-largest river in the country and the main river of the American Southwest.

THE COLORADO RIVER HEADWATERS

CHAPTER 9

Silver and Gold!

Names can tell us a lot about a place. From its name, we know that Colorado is colorful. From the valley, the mesa, and the plains, we know that Colorado is both "grand" and "great."

Years ago, the Rocky Mountains might have seemed too rocky and mountainous to be of much good to anyone, but they held a secret deep under the ground.

Some old mining towns are tourist attractions today.

PANNING FOR GOLD

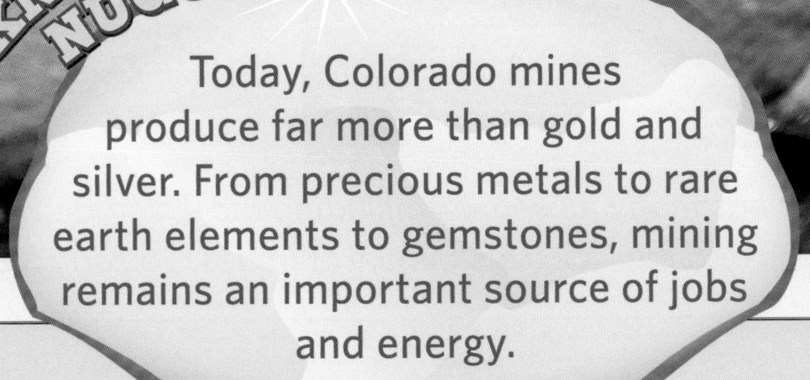

KNOWLEDGE NUGGET

Today, Colorado mines produce far more than gold and silver. From precious metals to rare earth elements to gemstones, mining remains an important source of jobs and energy.

A modern-day gold mine goes deep into the earth.

That secret brought many people to Colorado. The city of Golden, at the base of the mountains, is one clue to that treasure. The towns of Silver Cliff, Silver Plume, and Silverton are others.

Golden has many museums, including the Colorado Railroad Museum and the Colorado School of Mines Geology Museum.

Colorado was not yet a state when gold was discovered in 1858. The news set off a **frenzy** of excitement called a gold rush. Some 100,000 people hurried to the territory between 1859 and 1861 with dreams of striking it rich. Mining camps grew into towns. Towns grew into cities. In 1876, the territory became a state.

The discovery of silver followed a similar pattern. Lying deep below the land's surface were other valuable metals and minerals as well, such as copper, lead, and zinc. Today, mining is an important industry in Colorado.

Silverton is an old mining town located high in the San Juan Mountains.

CHAPTER 10

Energy Resources

WRANGLE UP SOME FACTS

In 2014, a Colorado utility company began building a $200 million large-scale solar power generating facility.

Other treasures lie beneath the state's surface. Coal and natural gas come from deep within the earth. These fuels are burned to produce electricity for the state. Colorado relies on coal more than any other **energy resource**. However, the state's coal industry is producing less coal than it once did. In 2013, Colorado was the eleventh-largest coal-producing state in the country.

A COAL MINER AT WORK

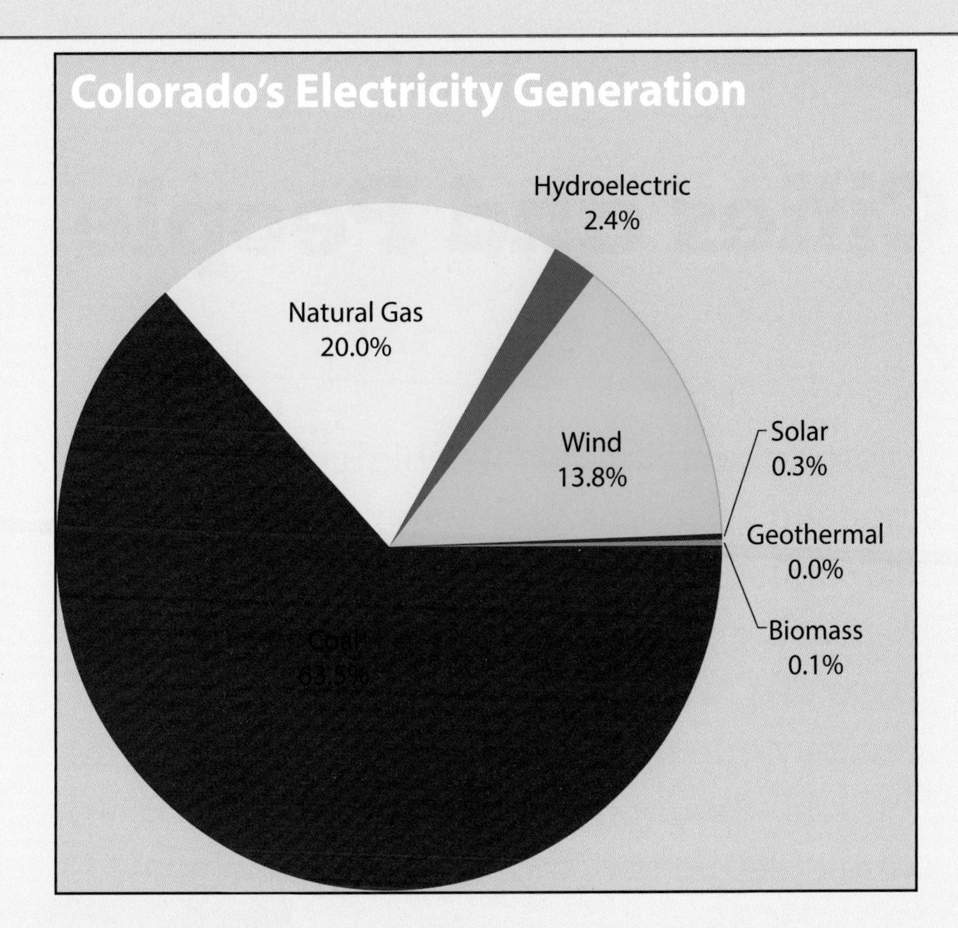

Traditional sources of energy, such as coal, oil, and natural gas, are called **fossil fuels**. These resources will not last forever. Therefore, the state also produces power from **renewable resources**. "Renewable" means these resources will not run out. Wind, sun (solar), and rushing river waters (**hydroelectric**) are some renewable resources. **Geothermal** processes use Earth's heat to produce energy. **Biomass** energy burns materials from plants. These methods are new, but may be Colorado's main energy sources of the future.

OUR POWER SOURCES

As you can see in the pie chart, by far most of Colorado's energy is produced by burning coal. New energy sources such as solar, geothermal, and biomass account for just a sliver of today's energy production.

Why might wind power be popular in this state?

CHAPTER 11

Cities and People

TWO-MILE-HIGH CITY
Leadville is the highest city in the United States at 10,430 feet (3,179 m).

Colorado's capital city lies high above most other state capitals. Denver is called the Mile-High City, and it really is a mile high in elevation! Its official elevation, or height above sea level, is 5,280 feet (1,609 m). That is precisely one mile. In fact, the Colorado State Capitol building has a marker on its 15th step to indicate the spot that is exactly one mile (1.6 km) high.

DENVER, THE STATE CAPITAL

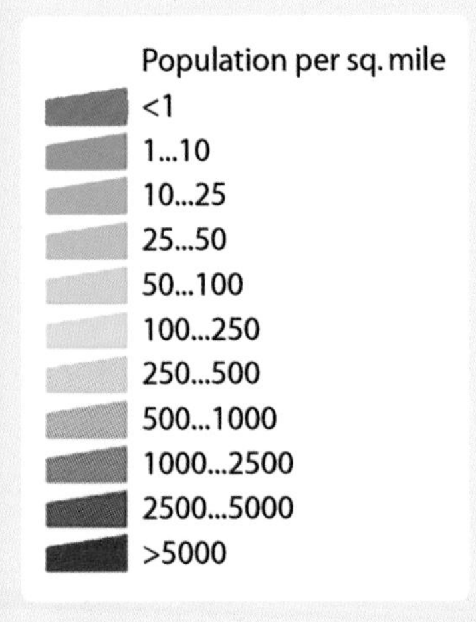

This map shows the population density of Colorado. The red areas have more than 5,000 people per square mile; dark green areas are the least populated.

Like many Colorado cities, Denver began as a mining town in the gold rush days. It is located where the High Plains meet the Front Range of the Rocky Mountains. A long, narrow strip of land runs north to south through Colorado between the plains and the mountains. Called the Front Range Urban Corridor, it means "city strip" or "city pathway." Instead of being scattered around the state, most of Colorado's main cities are located along this up-and-down line.

Boulder is frequently ranked "best city" in many categories: for its outdoor lifestyle, natural beauty, public transportation system, higher education, arts, and food.

COLORADO SPRINGS

Colorado Springs, Fort Collins, Pueblo, Boulder, Greeley, and many other cities and towns are located in this corridor. In fact, about 4,500,000 people live here. That's by far most of Colorado's population of 5 million or so. The rest of the state must seem a bit empty by comparison—or at least a lot less crowded!

Why might most people live in the urban corridor? Consider such factors as water, climate, the land, jobs, and other resources.

A girl creates a colorful scene in the Denver Chalk Art Festival.

FORT COLLINS

Fort Collins was the inspiration for the design of Main Street, USA, the "themed land" just inside the entrance to all the Disney parks around the world.

Coloradans are people of many different backgrounds. They are Native Americans, African Americans, white, Hispanic, and Asian Americans. All kinds of people worked hard to build this state. Everyone, past and present, is part of Colorado's story.

The Pearl Street Mall in downtown Boulder

CHAPTER 12

Protecting the Land

Coloradans know it's important to preserve the environment of their beautiful state. They have set aside hundreds of **conservation** areas to protect their land, wildlife, and historical sites. These special areas include national parks, trails, forests, and wildlife refuges, which are managed by the federal government. There are also many state and local parks and wildlife areas. All these places exist to protect the natural environment in its original condition. What

ROCKY MOUNTAIN NATIONAL PARK

The ancient dwellings are sheltered by the overhanging cliff.

would happen to Colorado if people could build factories, malls, and landfills anywhere at all?

Mesa Verde National Park, for example, is in Colorado's southwestern corner. About 1,500 years ago, native people called the Ancestral Puebloans lived here. They lived in caves and outcroppings they had carved out of the cliffs. About 600 such dwellings remain at this site. It's

KNOWLEDGE NUGGET

To see the cliff dwellings at Mesa Verde, you have to walk down about 100 steps and a series of ladders; then you have to walk back up!

BLACK CANYON NATIONAL PARK

the largest preserve of an ancient civilization in the United States.

The Black Canyon of the Gunnison National Park is another protected place. It preserves the extraordinary natural landscape of the Black Canyon in western Colorado. Rocky Mountain National Park in the Front Range of the Rockies

WELL PRESERVED

The Florissant Fossil Beds National Monument in Divide, Colorado, features groves of petrified redwood forests and thousands of fossilized insects. About 35 million years ago, volcanic eruptions covered this area in ash and lava, encasing plants and animals in stone.

A PLACE TO CALL HOME

The Alamosa Wildlife Refuge is 11,169 acres (4,520 ha) of wetland in southern Colorado. It supports songbirds, water birds, raptors, deer, beaver, and coyotes.

includes the Continental Divide. It's also the location of the headwaters of the Colorado River. Great Sand Dunes National Park and Preserve in the San Luis Valley protects a very different sort of environment. This park contains the tallest sand dunes in North America.

These and many other parks and refuges protect the land, animals, and majestic views of Colorado now and for the future.

WRANGLE UP SOME FACTS

OUCH!
The sand of the Great Sand Dunes can reach 140°F (60°C) on a summer afternoon.

GREAT SAND DUNES NATIONAL PARK

CHAPTER 13

Where the Wildlife Roam

Of the many animals that call Colorado home, the North American bison is one that is often associated with this region. Millions of bison, or buffalo, once roamed the western ranges. But in the 19th century, European settlers hunted the animals to near extinction. Today, thanks to national, state, and private conservation efforts, the species has been rescued. But the bison no longer live in the wild. A fraction of the old herds now graze in protected national parks and private reserves.

IT'S OFFICIAL!
The Rocky Mountain bighorn sheep was chosen to be the official state animal in 1961. These animals are found only in the Rockies.

BISON

Although these massive mammals are often called buffalo, that name is not quite right. True buffalo are native to Asia. Our "buffalo" are actually North American bison.

Bison roam on a ranch in the San Luis Valley.

Moose, bear, elk, bighorn sheep, and deer are some of the large mammals that do roam wild in the state. Mountain lions, coyote, and red foxes are present as well. Occasionally, hikers are hurt by wild animals, especially bears.

Colorado Parks and Wildlife professionals work with the public to teach them how to live safely with these animals. Importantly, the parks officials also work to protect the animals from people!

Colorado is home to the largest elk herd in the world, with some 280,000 elk. A century ago, there were fewer than 2,000 in the state.

HERD OF ELK

Glossary

alpine—relating to or characteristic of very high mountains

biomass—organic matter (remains of living things), which can be used as a fuel

canyon—a deep valley with steep cliffs on both sides; often has a river running through it

conservation—the protection of the natural environment

energy resource—anything that can be used as a source of power to make things work—such as run machines, provide heat, or make electricity

fossil fuels—natural fuels such as coal or gas, formed millions of years ago from the remains of living things

frenzy—a period of wild excitement

geothermal—relating to Earth's natural internal heat, which can be used as a source of energy

headwaters—the place where a river or stream begins

hydroelectric—electricity made by using flowing water (typically from a dammed-up river) to drive a turbine (a revolving machine) that powers a generator (a machine that converts energy into electricity)

mesa—a flat-topped mountain with steep sides

peak—the pointed top of a mountain

renewable resources—any resource, such as wood or solar energy, that can or will be replenished naturally over time

terrain—the ground, an area of land with certain physical features

tributary—a branch of a river; a smaller river or stream that flows into a larger river or lake

watershed—an area of land where all the water that lies under it, or drains off of it, flows to the same place

Index

Due to the changing nature of Internet links, the Rosen Publishing Group, Inc., has developed an online list of websites related to the subject of this book. This site is updated regularly. Please use this link to access the list: http://www.powerkidslinks.com/soco/lrc